ALL OUR
FARE-THEE-WELLS

poems by

Robert Cooperman

Finishing Line Press
Georgetown, Kentucky

ALL OUR FARE-THEE-WELLS

For Beth,
"My summer love for the spring, fall and winter"

Copyright © 2020 by Robert Cooperman
ISBN 978-1-64662-368-6 First Edition
All rights reserved under International and Pan-American Copyright Conventions. No part of this book may be reproduced in any manner whatsoever without written permission from the publisher, except in the case of brief quotations embodied in critical articles and reviews.

ACKNOWLEDGMENTS

The author is grateful to the editors of these journals, in which the following poems first appeared, sometimes in an earlier form:

Dead Matters: "Watching the Last Show Ever of the Grateful Dead: Pay Per View TV"
Nerve Cowboy: "At the University of Colorado Spine Center"
The Pangolin Review: "Selfies on the Plane"
The Program of the Grateful Dead Caucus: "Ask Amy"
Song of the San Joaquin Quarterly: "The License Plate"
Waterways: "The Little Old Lady in the Woodstock T-Shirt," "Hemingway, Garcia, or Santa"

Publisher: Leah Maines
Editor: Christen Kincaid
Cover Art: Grateful Dead—Denver, CO 1976 by SongLyrics on Flickr
Author Photo: Beth Cooperman
Cover Design: Elizabeth Maines McCleavy

Order online: www.finishinglinepress.com
　　　　　also available on amazon.com

Author inquiries and mail orders:
Finishing Line Press
P. O. Box 1626
Georgetown, Kentucky 40324
U. S. A.

Table of Contents

Ask Amy 1
Light Shows 2
Listening to the Grateful Dead at the Old Fillmore East 3
At the Civil War Battlefield of Antietam: Summer, 1988 4
The Dead Play Baltimore Memorial Stadium, 1988 5
Seeing the Grateful Dead, RFK Stadium, July, 1993 6
At Dunkin' Donuts, After a Grateful Dead Concert: Baltimore 7
Watching the Last Show Ever of the Grateful Dead: Pay Per
    View TV 8
At the Natural Foods Grocers, Denver 9
Selfies on the Plane 10
The Little Old Lady in the Woodstock T-Shirt 11
Winter Cold 12
At the University of Colorado Spine Center 13
In Our Dreams 14
Hemingway, Garcia, or Santa 16
In Sunny's Army-Navy Surplus Store 17
The License Plate 18
The Grateful Dead Dancing Terrapins Baseball Cap 19
The MRI Machine 20
Were You a Hippie? 21
A Fantasy of Taking My Great Niece to 710 Ashbury Street:
    San Francisco 22
We're Everywhere 23
A Question in the Buchtel Boulevard Post Office:
    Denver, Colorado 24
Music 25
Deciding Whether to Attend the Dead and Company Concert
    in Boulder 26

"Ask Amy"

My wife and I read
Amy's advice columns
over breakfast.

Today, a woman's hurt
that her brother will attend
a rock concert, and not
her 65th birthday party.

"Unless," Amy replies,
"that gig involves
Jerry Garcia returning
from the Other Side,
your brother has no excuse."

How many times
have I fantasized
the ghost of Garcia
flicking off riffs
of purest pearl,
and in fine, soulful voice
on my old favorites
and tunes he composed
during his sojourn
in the great Music Studio
in the Sky?

But rather than dwell
on what can't ever be,
Beth and I look at each other
when I finish the article,
and laugh as heartily
as Garcia might've.

Light Shows

Most pulsed colors onto the screen
at the Fillmore East; but one—
when the Dead launched into
"Dark Star," twenty-three minutes
of psychedelic epiphanies—

flashed a travelogue of a convertible
tooling down desert blacktops,
the driver's elbow resting
on the rolled down window well,
an utterly nonchalant forefinger
on the wheel, his freak flag
a symbol of America, where nothing's
as satisfying as driving far and fast.

The piece picked up steam and speed,
and the ragtop zoomed into space,
dancing past the moon, red Mars,
weaving in and out of Saturn's rings,
then leaving stars behind, strange planets,
and on and on into deeper space,
until "Dark Star" concluded.

Not waiting for applause to detonate,
the band soared into "St. Stephen,"
all of us roaring for the music to never end,

as all things must.

Listening to the Grateful Dead at the Old Fillmore East

We listened with our ears and bodies too,
otherwise known as dancing to music
that got into each muscle and sinew,

into our bones and our blood, and corkscrewed
us into dervishes on pogo sticks,
dancing with our ears, and our bodies too,

while the Dead slowed the tempo, then frenzy-flew
with nothing more than a harmonic flick
that got into each muscle and sinew.

It felt like we'd been transported right through
the Fillmore's roof on a spaceship joystick,
hearing with our ears, and our bodies too.

But the Dead finished before we were through
dancing, twirling to the wild kinetic:
vibrating in each muscle and sinew,

so when dawn pinked on Second Avenue,
we ambled home, on fire and sweat-slick,
entranced with our ears and our bodies too,
each muscle alive, each dancing sinew.

At the Civil War Battlefield at Antietam: Summer, 1988

A friend was in Baltimore
for a literary conference,
and to our delight spent her last two days
with Beth and me, but Cora had brought
nothing casual to wear, and since
she's a raised fist taller than Beth,
I lent her a Grateful Dead t-shirt,
for our tour of Antietam.

In the parking lot, a kid was firing
his cap rifle at everyone and laughing
to see them jump, to fling Cora into a rage
and Beth and me to beg her to keep still,
reasoning nothing good ever came
of dissing a kid in front of his parents,
no matter how much the brat deserved it.

"Too many men have died here,"
Cora's snarl froze the kid, and us,
"for you to be playing with a gun."
And as I'd feared, the father detonated:

"Listen, Commie, anyone wearing anything
praising those degenerates should shut up!"

To which, Cora shouted, "Fascist!
At least they never murdered anyone,
which I wouldn't be surprised
you gleefully brag about,"

while the kid's mother hid her perp-walk face,
and Beth and I coaxed Cora away
before he pulled a live piece: how real
Americans settle disputes, amid the graves.

The Dead Play Baltimore Memorial Stadium, 1990

Two young friends are visiting,
Malaysian students of Beth's,
about to start their careers,
and curious about
everything American.

"What can we show them
that's typical of America?"
Beth demands, and I remember
the Grateful Dead is playing
in Baltimore tonight and tomorrow:
and if they aren't American as apple pie—
seasoned with maybe a lid of grass—
then I don't know what is.

After our friends' long drive,
I ask if they'd like to see the Dead.
Their foreheads furrow like Zen
sand garden rake marks
depicting a typhoon,
since they fear the name,
the Grateful Dead, means
a Satanic ritual,

until I explain the folktale.

So I call the box office,
but the shows have been sold out
for weeks, Winson assuaging
his disappointment by saying
they have all the time in the world.

But only a year later, at
"With-his-whole-life-in-front of-him
age of twenty-six," his heart
sent him on his journey
to join the sainted dead.

Seeing the Grateful Dead, RFK Stadium, July, 1993

Twenty years since I'd seen them,
but now, with friends in the gathering
dusk, kids dancing on the infield,
our upper deck seats shuddering
with our stomping feet, twirling hips,

it hit me like feedback
from an amp the size of Maryland
that I couldn't pick out Jerry Garcia
from the other musicians onstage;
Charles pointed to a t-shirted grizzly.

"My God," I murmured, "he must weigh
300 pounds. What happened?"

"Fast food and heroin."

"Shouldn't smack have at least
canceled out the calories?" I wondered.

"The world's stranger," Charles shrugged,
"than you or I can imagine."

"Jesus, he's a wreck," I said,
frightened for a favorite uncle,
though his fingers flew
along the frets, and tunes filled the air,

two years before he went still
and silent forever.

At Dunkin' Donuts, After a Grateful Dead Concert: Baltimore

Still high from weed and the music soaring
off the stage at D.C.'s RFK Stadium,
whistling tunes driving back to Baltimore,
we stopped at a Dunkin' Donuts near our house,
all of us hungry and too wired to sleep.
The counterwoman tried to smile at paying customers,
but hard to perform that trick of the lips
at the tail end of a graveyard shift.

Just then, in burst a woman in hot-pink hot pants,
a guy striding behind her, the two of them shouting:
half the customers groaning, "Not again,"
the other half sitting up, alert for entertainment.
She accused he didn't look out for her interests
so she was leaving him, and he spat "You ain't
going nowhere, bitch," though it didn't sound
anything like Dylan's love ballad of the same title.

And just when we feared he'd haul off and belt her
or worse, use the blade he was going for
in his pocket, he deflated, ordered a honey glazed
and a cup of coffee, and collapsed into a seat,
but too tired to take the first bite, while she sat
beside him and stroked the side of his face,
and he kissed her once, softly, on the cheek,
and rubbed her hand against his midnight stubble,

their sadness and rage vanished, at least for now.

Watching the Last Show Ever of the Grateful Dead: Pay Per View TV

Who could afford tickets and a hotel room?
Not us. So Beth and I settle for live TV
and not a joint or pipe: Beth frowning
on my imbibing, and nowadays, my lungs
rasp like stripped-down gears, after one toke.

The concert's a treat, though if we're honest,
we admit something's missing: Garcia,
gone twenty years, but still indispensable,
though his vocals were nothing Tony Bennett
need feel threatened by. Still, they fit the music
like a Dancing Bears t-shirt and broken-in jeans.

As for his guitar solos, a bounce we don't hear
in this technically perfect performance,
but let's not quibble: this is as close as we'll get
ever again to seeing the real-live Grateful Dead.

After the camera scans the crowd—balloons
bouncing, smoke blown like giant gnat swarms,
Bill Walton's big goofy grin and peace signs—
it focuses on the stage, and despite knowing
he's gone, a small part of me expects to see Garcia,
not the heroin-wreck, but the young guy who epiphanied,

"Hey, I can make a living doing what I love."

And then the show's over, the crowd shuffles out,
the stage empties, all our fare-thee-wells sung and said.

At the Natural Foods Grocers, Denver

While the young cashier rings me up,
she keeps glancing at my baseball cap,
with its imprint of Jerry Garcia,
gone more than twenty years now,
though a lot of us still remember him
and his music that lifted us to heaven.

I can see she wants to ask about the image,
maybe inquire, "Is that Jerry Garcia?"
or more likely, "Who's that?"

I smile encouragement, but she just hands me
my change, and I amble out, store my purchases
in our fridge, then decide since it's Monday,
to walk to Anthony's Pizza, maybe the best
slices west of the Hudson.

While I wait for Al to hand me my change,
he asks, "You got your tickets for the Dead
and Company Show yet?" I tell him Beth and I
are betting it'll be on pay per view, cheaper,
and no need to drive home early in the morning,
on a dark, twisty road under perpetual construction.

Al shrugs his disappointment at my lack
of commitment, but smiles at my cap,
and brings out my two slices: us Dead Heads
sticking together, or he's acknowledging that yes,
I'm too feeble to balance the plates without falling
face down into scalding, fragrant pizza sauce.

Selfies on the Plane

The young, attractive couple
in the row ahead of ours,
can't stop snapping themselves
and admiring their good looks.
But in two shots, there I am,
between them, with my
Jerry Garcia baseball cap,
without even realizing
I'd cuckooed into their shot.

Embarrassed to bogart
their private moments,
I turn to watch the sunset
with Beth: sky darkening
into crimson, then narrowing,
as gray, then black-night,
elbows out the evening's
gorgeously dying colors.

I return to the book
I'm not really enjoying,
but glance at that couple again,
flicking through their selfies;
and there I am: a geezer
with a baseball cap's likeness
of a rock star who died
more than twenty years ago.

I wouldn't be insulted
if they deleted Jerry and me,
but they don't, maybe sensing
he's watching, the plane
this close to Heaven.

The Little Old Lady in the Woodstock T-Shirt

I spot her in the Safeway parking lot,
at least 80 and hanging onto her shopping cart
as if teetering with vertigo at a cliff's edge,
her cane resting on the cart's handle.

On her t-shirt, the Woodstock symbol:
birds trilling on a guitar's frets,
Love and Peace in the grass-aromatic air,
while her cart totters with the blind
staggers to her Bug that she trembles open.

"Can I help you, Ma'am?" I ask,
as she struggles to lift her shopping bag
as if a barbell, and drops the dead weight
into the back seat.

She stares at me, as if afraid
I'll hit her over the head for her purse
she grips like a lifeline, which maybe it is:
with all her money, I.D., and credit cards.

She looks at me again, notes my beard,
what's left of my hair gathered in a ponytail,
sees my Jerry Garcia t-shirt, and demands,

"Wanna score some righteous shit?
If not, get the fuck outta my face."

Winter Cold

Fittingly, while I hack and wheeze,
I'm wearing the Grateful Dead hoodie
my wife gave me for my birthday:

the skulls and skeletons two more symbols,
as if I need them, that this life is fleeting
and filled with pain, or in my case,

the annoyance of coughing spasms,
while my nostrils flow like broken mains,
and I drink enough water, juices, and lemon tea

to consider inventing a tube to connect me
to the toilet bowl; my body and those skeletons
and acid-grinning skulls are telling me

to take it easy, read, watch mindless TV,
and keep on truckin', but in slow motion,
or just sleep, which eluded me last night,

my wife murmuring, "Poor baby,"
every time I heaved up from bed,
not feeling grateful for anything.

At the University of Colorado Hospital Spine Center

The spine doctor's a dead ringer
for all the women I knew back
at Brooklyn College in the late '60s:
waist length folksong-black hair,
a New York twang thick as pastrami,
a Grateful Dead sweatshirt, flannel
skin-tights, and red Converse high tops.

So I trust she won't take one glance
at my MRI and X-ray and announce,

"We operate in ten minutes; last requests?"

Instead, she points to eroded disks,
but also to where the spine is still healthy.
Then, in the nasal Brooklynese I've not
lost either, she lists the possibilities;
we decide on an epidural shot in my spine.

"This may or may not work," she advises,
"but there's other options before we have
to think surgery," though she also warns
the shot may not erase all my pain.

Still, it's nice to dream of walking,
even slowly, around the park's lakes,
and not teeter and tap with my cane,
while listening to the ghosts
of Jerry Garcia and Pigpen
harmonize on an old blues number,

when my generation believed
its birthright was to stay forever young.

In Our Dreams

In my dream last night,
I was the great Elgin Baylor,
going up and up for the elegant bucket
I was about to score, hanging
like a balloon in mid-air, softly
banking the ball into the hissing net,
to wild applause, the shrieking
disbelief of the announcer.

When I hit the floor again, panic
grabbed me like a mugger: terrified
I'd ruined my real-life just-replaced hip.
I woke, my breaths like a failing
locomotive on a mountain incline.

Far more pleasant: the other night,
Beth dreamed we were cousins
to Jerry Garcia, who'd dropped by
to play some tunes and give us tickets
to a concert.

My cousin's daughter will be married
August 9th, the day Garcia died; I won't
mention that to anyone at the wedding,
nor the even worse commemoration:
the 70th dreadful anniversary of Nagasaki.

Instead, I'll laugh with family I've not seen
in far too many years, eat too many canapés,
drink a little too much, and maybe later,
in the hotel bed, I'll dream of Jerry
playing at the old Fillmore East:

in rare form on "Dark Star"
and "New Minglewood Blues,"
his fingers inventing riffs
never even dreamed of;
and the light show: a highlight reel
of Elgin's greatest moves.

Hemingway, Garcia, or Santa

He walks toward me
as I head for a bagel shop;
and a part of me, puckish

as Shakespeare's sprite,
is tempted to ask of his
polar-bear luxuriant beard,

"So who are you: Ernest, Jerry,
or Santa?" But he's big
as that polar bear: a biker,

with a skull and crossbones
t-shirt stretched over a stomach
bellying out like a ship's keel.

I offer a smile wan as a moth
and enter, for my daily fix:
an onion bagel, and a chocolate

chip cookie for Beth and me to share.
Whoever he was—Hemingway,
Garcia, or Santa Claus—

he's disappeared when I walk out:
not even the fading roar of a Harley:
nor guitar riffs soaring into the air,

nor whip cracks and calls of,
"On Prancer!" gifts tumbling
from his overstuffed sack.

In Sunny's Army-Navy Surplus Store

There's more ink on the arms of employees
and guys shopping for camping equipment,
work clothes, and Bowie blades bigger
and sharper than Highland broad swords,
than in all the illuminations in The Book of Kels.

A good thing, in my desperation for new jeans
to replace the ones that look grizzly-gnawed,
that I haven't worn my Jerry Garcia baseball cap
or I'd probably be stuffed into the alley-Dumpster.
I try to swagger and spit curses like a real man,
not hum a song or read from the book I'm seldom
without, in case checkout lines are too long.

But the young woman at the counter smiles
at my purchases, as if carpenter's jeans align me
with hard working men pissed off at everything
from the economy to billionaires to politicians,
especially the one they saw as a foreign-born,
Christ killing, blood sucking Islamo-terrorist.

As she hands me back my Visa card,
she reminds me not so much of a gun toting
low riding Democrat-hater, as the hippies
I knew so long ago they're almost as ancient
history as the Middle Ages: with her hair
in Pre-Raphaelite ringlets, her Indian blouse,
and earrings that could tinkle out a tune
by the Grateful Dead as she trucks down a street.

She thanks me for my purchase, I smile back,
pocket my card, my receipt, take my new jeans,
and imagine guys are staring at me, as if debating
whether to garrote, stab, stomp, or shoot me;
when I'm outside, I whistle a happy melody.

The License Plate

> *"GR8FUL-1"*
> —*License plate of a car on South Franklin Street, Denver*

I've just come from the post office,
buying Jimi Hendrix commemoratives,
and quipping to the clerk,

"So when can I expect the Jerry Garcias?"

"Yeah," he smiled, and wore that look
of bringing up the full lobster pot
of good musical memories, though
too young to have seen the band live.

A few minutes later, I'm driving
to pick up Beth at the light rail station,
the thin Denver air heavy with impending snow.
A Bug convertible wears a GR8FUL-1 plate,
coincidences building today like guitar riffs,
and I'm psychedelic green with envy
that I didn't think of it first.

I want to make a gesture he'd recognize
as a fellow Deadhead, but he turns left;
besides, I'm so old he might've taken
my raised fist of approbation
for shooting a neo-hippie the bird.

Better just to savor his plate, of tasting
the delights of once being young,
when we thought music could save the world,
or at least make it more bearable.

The Grateful Dead Dancing Terrapins Baseball Cap

The receptionist at this urgent care center
compliments my baseball cap when I sign in.

"Thanks," I smile, despite the urinary infection:
my urethra barbwire every time I piss.

"We're everywhere!" I chime the code
to a fellow Deadhead, but she throws a look

blank as the black boards I'd dusted
and washed, at after-school detention.

"Jerry Garcia?" the name, in my nostalgic universe,
should be clarification enough.

"Who?" her young brow's furrowed, as if considering
the most confusing math problem ever devised.

"The Grateful Dead?" though I should just wish her
a nice day, grip my prescription, and leave.

"Oh right," she smiles, humoring an ex-hippie geezer,
and probably thinking I'm in league with the devil,

or at the least, plan to dig up some graves
in the local cemetery one dark night, soon,

and conduct unspeakable experiments.

The MRI Machine

I ram in the earplugs for my ride
into this claustrophobic torpedo tube
that'll show me how bad my spine is,
and whether I need dreaded surgery.

Twenty minutes, the tech promises,
and hands me an escape button,
if I can't bear the noise
or if the machine's walls close in
like those crushing rooms
in old cliffhanger serials.

With the earplugs in place, I think,

"Hell, this isn't so bad,"
until the hammering starts:
the world's loudest punk band
smashing one note over and over.

Finally, I'm free, and I can't wait
to see my wife, patient to help me
hobble to our Toyota, where I'll crank
up the Grateful Dead's joyful noise,

proof I'm not dead yet.

Were You a Hippie?

"Were you a hippie, Uncle Bob?"
my nephew asked me decades ago.
Before I could answer: yes, no, maybe,
Beth shot me a look of,

"Don't you dare mention drugs!"

"No Alby," I kidded, "I didn't like
yogurt or honey, so I was barred from
the Hippie Union," his forehead
a furrow of, "Huh?" at a concert
the summer after Jerry Garcia died.

Two decades later, Alby's a public
defender, proving a man couldn't
have committed a murder, no matter
how badly the state wanted to kill the guy.

Over dinner, he describes his latest case,
and asks us not to talk about it, except
he says that once again, the prosecution
is dying to kill an innocent man.

Sort of like the army: salivating
to toss a generation of us into the jungle
and let us get shot or go nuts there.

A Fantasy of Taking Our Great Niece to 710 Ashbury Street: San Francisco

We'll meet Lylah and her mother
in the City by the Bay later in the year,
and while Oakleigh's presenting
a paper at an international conference,
Beth and I will take our great niece
to 710 Ashbury Street, to initiate her
into the one true religion:
the Grateful Dead.

It's been a decade since we visited
that holy portal and took photos,
and believed we'd heard tunes still
drifting through the windows and walls.

I imagine Lylah scrunching up her nose
as if at an unpleasant odor, and asking,

"Uncle Bob, why did they call
themselves that? It's kinda creepy."

I'll tell her how Garcia found
the term, and how it's an old folktale,

"A fairytale," I'll tell Lylah,
still young enough to believe in them.
And it is a great story: of repaying debts
from beyond the grave. Besides,
the telling never fails to raise a smile:
that there's redemption, maybe salvation,
even for an old reprobate like me.

We're Everywhere

I've accompanied my wife
to her university's fund raiser.
While sampling a buffet dish
I couldn't pronounce
with a gun to my head, this guy—
wearing a suit that costs more
than our car—asks my profession.

"A poet," I cringe
at the condescension
about to slap my face.

"Got a book published?"
I nod.

"What about?" he demands.

"My latest? The Grateful Dead,"
and wait for his sneer.

Instead, he confides,

"I wept like a baby
when Jerry died,"
and while we reminisce
about shows and songs,
we're joined by my wife's dean,
who asks what we're talking about,
his accent makes Daniel Day Lewis
sound like Tony Soprano.

"The Dead?" he gushes,
"I listen to them all the time,"
the three of us nodding
to the music in our heads:
the delicacies on our plates
growing cold.

A Question in the Buchtel Boulevard Post Office: Denver, Colorado

"So when can I expect
the Jerry Garcia stamps?"
I'll ask every now and then,
half in jest, half because I want
to stare at Jerry's Cheshire face,

like I used to cast loving looks
at the Willie Mays outfielder's glove
in the window of the local
sporting goods store.

The last time, Eddie—
with whom I've bantered
about Garcia whenever I step up
to his station, spat—

"A stamp honoring that junkie?"
so I know something's personal,
and don't shoot back,

"Jimi and Janis didn't O.D.?"
since he's rhapsodized about
those commemorated rock stars,

not to mention his love for Elvis,
dead on his Graceland commode
and flying on only God, or Satan,
knew what was racing
like vicious rats through his veins.

Music

> *"We need music. I don't know why. We need magic, and bliss, and power, myth, and celebration and religion in our lives. And music is a good way to encapsulate a lot of it."*
> —Jerry Garcia

Especially in these terrible times
we need music to drown out all the guns,
all the shouting hatred, and all the lies.

Some simple truths, instead, in chords and rhymes,
melodies meant to comfort, like hot Cross buns,
especially in these terrible times,

with vitriol-grenades and hate-landmines;
and triggers pulled, as if in good, clean fun,
the consequences of bile-shouted lies.

We need tunes on which we can harmonize,
join arms and sway in breezes in the sun.
Yes, Kumbayah in these terrible times.

Lovely music to send chills down our spines:
something that charms, when all is said and done,
and drowns out the savage hatred and lies.

Jerry, how I wish you were still alive
and singing and flicking off guitar runs,
to bring me some joy in these dreadful times,
and not have to hear the guns and the lies.

Deciding Whether to Attend the Dead and Company Concert in Boulder

Three surviving members of the Grateful
Dead, along with special musical guests,
so Beth and I talk it over, and sadly decide
it's too much of a schlep to drive up there,
then drive home or spend the night in a motel
and besides, neither of us loves crowds anymore,
and Beth's allergic to weed whiff, though I still
inhale, when I scent someone toking up.

We're pretty sure it'll be streaming soon,
way cheaper than seats at Folsom Field,
and we can see better on TV, like NBA games,
where even at center court, the action's a blur.

Besides, we're getting too old for this,
not like when we thought nothing
of boogying all night with the Dead.

"Now if Jerry's ghost were to show up,"
I joke to Beth, "or if the man himself
were still alive, that'd change everything,"

like all those hopeful sightings of Elvis.

Robert Cooperman is a graduate of the joint Creative Writing and Literature Ph.D. program at the University of Denver. Among his awards and credits is wining the Colorado Book Award for Poetry in 2000, for *In the Colorado Gold Fever Mountains* (Western Reflections Books). In addition, Cooperman was runner up for the Women Writing the West WILLA Award, for *The Widow's Burden* (also Western Reflections Books). More recently, Cooperman's *My Shtetl* won the Holland Award from Logan House Press. *Draft Board Blues* (FutureCycle Press) was named One of the Ten Best Reads by a Colorado Author for 2017, by *WestWord Magazine* of Denver. In all, Cooperman has published more than twenty full-length collections and six previous chapbooks, most recently among his full-length collections are two inspired by *The Odyssey: Lost on the Blood-Dark Sea* (FutureCycle Press), a retelling of the epic poem; and *The Ghosts and Bones of Troy* (Kelsay Books), which posits, what if Odysseus returned to Ithaca with a horrific case of what we'd now call PTSD.

The impetus for *All Our Fare-Thee-Wells* grew out of Cooperman's lifelong love (some might accuse it's an obsession, especially friends and family he's forced to listen to hours of their songs and jams) with the Grateful Dead. The band's music has seen him through bad times and floated him to the gates of heaven during good times. This chapbook is the fourth collection for which Cooperman has used the music and/or the medieval folktale from which the band took its name. And, he hopes, it won't be the last.

Cooperman lives with his wife Beth in Denver.

www.ingramcontent.com/pod-product-compliance
Lightning Source LLC
LaVergne TN
LVHW041518070426
835507LV00012B/1669